Original title:
Shadows and Sassafras

Copyright © 2025 Creative Arts Management OÜ
All rights reserved.

Author: Samuel Kensington
ISBN HARDBACK: 978-1-80567-193-0
ISBN PAPERBACK: 978-1-80567-492-4

Clandestine Paths Through Time

In a world where secrets live,
The squirrels conspire and give.
Whispers float, a giggling breeze,
As acorns plot with utmost ease.

Beneath the surface, tales unfold,
Of mischief brewed from legends old.
A dance of jest, a twirl of glee,
As shadows waltz, carefree and free.

The Tapestry of Sinking Sunlight

Golden threads of mischief weave,
Through the twilight, jokes conceive.
A wink from the sun, a sly goodbye,
Leaving giggles that float and fly.

Molasses laughter drips down trees,
As breezes tease with playful ease.
We chase the glow, in shades of mirth,
Crafting joy upon this earth.

A Tangle of Time and Memory

Twisted yarns of yesteryears,
Untangle laughter, hide the tears.
Each knot a story, silly and bright,
Binding us in the soft twilight.

With every tug, a chuckle springs,
As laughter dances, the heartstrings sing.
Mischief waits in every loop,
In a merry, whimsical troop.

Rustling Leaves of Forgotten Lore

Leaves murmur secrets, old yet new,
Tickling ears with a playful view.
Fables bounce in the crisp, cool air,
With whispers of nonsense that dare to flare.

Giggles rustle in the golden hues,
As laughter sprinkles like morning dew.
The forest knows how to have fun,
In its embrace, we all become one.

Whispers of the Gloaming

In corners dark where giggles creep,
The cat's got secrets, wouldn't you peep?
With silly hats and pirate tales,
The moonlight jests, while the owl wails.

Beneath the trees, the raccoons dance,
In two left paws, they take a chance.
A twist of fate with a wobbly spin,
As fireflies join in with a cheeky grin.

The Secrets of Fading Light

Lurking around with mischief's delight,
The gnomes play pranks in the dimming light.
With wobbly legs and a sly little grin,
They trade their hats for a tumbleweed spin.

On branches high, the squirrels debate,
Who's got more acorns? Oh, isn't it great?
A chuckle escapes from a sly, furry face,
In this twilight world, it's all just a race.

Echoes in the Twilight Grove

The trees chuckle softly, the breeze gives a sigh,
As owls tell tales, and the crickets reply.
With shadows that giggle and leap on the ground,
Waving goodnight to the stars all around.

A rustle, a shuffle, what's that in the brush?
It's just a young rabbit, in quite a big rush!
With twitching nose and no time to halt,
He'd eaten the flowers and blames it on salt.

Beneath the Canopy of Mystery

When dusk takes the stage, and the stars come alive,
Bugs don their shades and the fireflies jive.
With laughter like bubbles that burst in the air,
A party for critters, the forest's affair.

The hedgehogs wear ties, the badgers all cheer,
As chuckles and snickers fill up the sphere.
In shadows of giggles, they dance till the dawn,
In this wild, wacky spot where silliness spawns.

Murmurs Amidst the Understory

In the thicket where whispers creep,
Bouncing laughs make the critters leap.
Leaves exchange secrets, oh what a sight,
As light dances through the branches' delight.

Look out for the squirrel with shades so cool,
He's got them all raving, 'Ain't nature a fool?'
With every hop, he shows off his flair,
While the rabbits just giggle, without a care.

Hints of Magic in the Air

A wily breeze tickles the trees,
Painting the leaves with whimsical tease.
Frogs in bow ties sing with glee,
While fireflies twirl like they own the spree.

One butterfly boasts of a magical feat,
As bees do the cha-cha, oh what a treat!
The mushrooms chime in, looking so spry,
With a wink and a nudge, they float by.

The Veins of Solitude

In the deep forest where thoughts can roam,
Beneath ferns, the lost get a temporary home.
Squirrels debate the best nut in town,
While owls take bets, wearing quite the frown.

A lone mushroom wears a tiny cap,
Sighing softly, 'Oh, where's my happy rap?'
As twilight approaches, the night grows sly,
Chasing away the echoes, oh me, oh my!

Underneath the Boughs of Mystery

Under twisted limbs, tales intertwine,
Where raccoons host parties, passing the wine.
With twinkling eyes, they tell of the night,
While owls provide music, just outta sight.

A dandelion dreams of flying high,
While a witty worm sings, 'Oh my, oh my!'
As laughter erupts from the depths of green,
Nature's own comedy, a lively scene.

The Language of Vanishing Veils

In a garden where giggles grow,
Whispers dance, twirling low.
Petals hide, secrets near,
A playful breeze sings, never fear.

Mischief winks from behind the trees,
Caught in the sway of the teasing breeze.
Tricksters play with hidden sights,
As moonlight wobbles, lost in flights.

Tales Told by Flickering Flames

Around the fire, stories leap,
With cackles and chuckles, never deep.
Embers glow with cheerful flair,
As shadows prance without a care.

The flames laugh at what we say,
As sparks swirl round in a merry way.
Grinning logs hold secrets bold,
While the night wraps us in a hold.

The Threads of Hidden Pathways

In a maze of giggles, we run wild,
With twists and turns that leave us smiled.
Each step a jest upon the ground,
With paths that giggle, twirl around.

Laughter echoes like a bell,
In corners where surprises dwell.
Tangled yarns of joy are spun,
As we chase mirth, just for fun.

Beneath the Crooked Boughs

Underneath branches, bent and neat,
We share our snacks, a delightful treat.
Boughs above whisper funny schemes,
While we craft our mischievous dreams.

Lively critters poke their heads,
Peeking at our giggles, not our breads.
With every laugh and wink in sight,
The world feels warm, and oh, so bright.

Leaves of Autumn's Secrets

Rustling leaves wear silly hats,
Chattering squirrels dance with bats.
A pumpkin grins with wicked charm,
While ghosts giggle, no cause for alarm.

Winds whisper jokes, a playful tease,
As acorns bounce from lofty trees.
The crisp air laughs, it takes a jab,
At all the critters in their fab.

Echoes of the Enchanted Grove

In the grove, the owls have flair,
With monocles and tales to share.
The trees gossip like giddy teens,
While mushrooms plot in their little greens.

Crickets chirp a quirky tune,
As fireflies light up like balloons.
The moon winks, it's quite the show,
As woodland creatures steal the glow.

Dance of the Sylvan Spirits

Spirits twirl in whimsical style,
Tickling toadstools all the while.
With twinkling eyes and peals of glee,
They throw a bash beneath the tree.

Breezes bounce, with a fluttering cheek,
Laughing at shadows that dare to peek.
With every step, the world ignites,
In this frolic of leafy delights.

Veiled in Verdant Hues

Green capes flutter on playful sprites,
Behind thick bushes, they spark delights.
With jests that echo through leafy halls,
And laughter that dances as nightfall calls.

Fern fronds wave in cheeky patterns,
While critters ponder on their matters.
A mischief here, a giggle there,
In hidden realms, joy fills the air.

The Play of Silhouettes and Light

In the park where phantoms dance,
The munchkins trip and prance.
Chasing tails that wander free,
Dodging trees like a game of spree.

Laughter echoes, sharp and bright,
As they spin in pure delight.
Every glance, a hidden jest,
While the sun sinks to the west.

Beneath the canopy's embrace,
Sillier forms take on a face.
Giggling at the playful tease,
As leaves flutter down with ease.

The evening wears a clever grin,
As the day lets laughter in.
Who needs gloom when we can sway,
In a world where fun leads the way?

The Echo of Timeless Whispers

Through the trees, a voice just squeaked,
"What's the gossip?" it intrigued.
The curls of twigs lean in to hear,
As squirrels hold their breath in cheer.

Secrets bounce on breezy trails,
Where antics reign and laughter prevails.
A wink from one to another,
Makes even daisies stutter.

With mischief brewing like a tea,
Tales of grand absurdity!
Each rustling leaf a chuckle bestowed,
On creatures with a silly code.

The wind tickles every branch,
Inviting all to join the dance.
A symphony of giggles flow,
Where whispers bloom and antics grow.

Layers of Enigma Beneath the Oak

Underneath the mighty oak,
Curious critters drift and poke.
With every rustle, what a sight,
A game of hide and seek ignites!

Rabbits leap in wild disguise,
As hedgehogs plot with twinkling eyes.
"Did you hear what badger said?"
A riddle wraps around their head.

The old roots wiggle with delight,
While shadows play in soft moonlight.
A chuckle from the wise old bark,
As laughter lingers in the dark.

Every branch holds quips and jests,
Crafted by the forest's guests.
With layers thick, the night unfolds,
As giggles turn to stories told.

The Intricacy of Night's Grasp

In the night where giggles loom,
With every glance, a hint of gloom.
Yet, owls hoot with flair and zest,
Inviting all to join the fest.

Under stars like playful eyes,
Mischief dances, oh what a surprise!
Creatures stir in the moonlit droves,
Where every corner playfully roves.

In the gardens of odd delights,
Caterpillars engage in flights.
A round of jokes, a secret quiz,
While the night steals the show with fizz.

Around each corner, peeks a grin,
As confusion reigns, we all jump in.
In the delicate grasp of night,
We find our giggles take to flight.

The Silhouette of Enchantment

In the corner, a figure pranced,
With a twirl and a sudden glance.
What nonsense, I hear them share,
As whispers tickle the evening air.

Moonlight spilled, it danced with flair,
A sprightly jig, no hint of care.
A giggle hid in the darkened space,
What mischief blooms in a merry place?

Through flittering giggles, all bright and spry,
A cheshire smile swept through the sky.
Who knew that the night could play so bold,
With tales of folly waiting to be told?

Our shadows juggled, they spun around,
In the laughter's grip, we all were found.
A riot of whimsy, a quilt of cheer,
Who needs the dawn? The night is here!

Gossamer Threads of Dusk

Beneath the beams, the laughter spun,
As tiny feet danced, oh what fun!
Velvet skies played peek-a-boo,
With tricksters ready for something new.

Lurking 'neath the lavender bloom,
A playful thrum dispelled the gloom.
Twirls and leaps, they stole the scene,
In a world of giggles, oh so keen!

Little voices called from the dark,
A riddle shared, a tantalizing spark.
What bane had the night set free?
Too much giggling to simply be.

Feathery whispers claimed the night,
As mischief brewed, oh what a sight!
In tangled yarns and gleeful chuckles,
Who knew dusk held such delightful luckles?

Secrets in the Underbrush

Beneath the leaves, where whispers dwell,
A saga blooms, oh can't you tell?
Fuzzy critters share a giggle,
As they dance and jump, and wiggle.

In a patch of earth, during twilight's gleam,
Mischief brews like a wild dream.
'Tis not the night that holds the game,
But the secrets wrapped in starlit fame.

Crouching low, the antics surprise,
Who knew grass could hold such highs?
With acorns tossed, and feathers floored,
In the undercut, the fun is stored.

These merry souls, a raucous crew,
Spin stories fresh, and laughter too.
In tangled worlds, where time may pause,
Oh, what hilarity without a cause!

Reflections of a Wistful Dream

In the gloam, where giggles swell,
A frolicsome tale bids all to dwell.
Clouds catch whispers, bright and clear,
With secrets tucked away, so near.

Fluttering thoughts on breezy wings,
Unraveled yarns of amusing things.
Each flicker twinkled, danced in flight,
Oh, who knew dreams could spark such light?

Through glimmers and grins, they twined and swayed,
In the weave of merriment, never frayed.
What jests await in the night's embrace?
With moonlit winks and a happy face!

Beneath the crescent's playful tease,
Surprises bloom like flowers in the breeze.
A canvas painted with laughter's stream,
Embracing the night, the sweetest dream!

Enigmas at Dusk

In the corner, a cat does plot,
With whiskers twitching in the not.
Chasing dust bunnies that tease and dart,
Sleuthing secrets, a feline art.

The lamp flickers, shadows prance,
A toddler giggles, takes a chance.
Wobbling under an oversized hat,
Be careful, dear! You'll squish the cat!

At twilight's whimsy, squirrels debate,
Who gets the acorn, who'll have fate?
With a pointed tail, they hurl and cheer,
Like a circus cast, it's all quite clear.

The riddle of the evening light,
Hilarity blooms, mirth takes flight.
Between the whispers and laughter's swell,
Comedic tales the dusk will tell.

The Dance of Dappled Dreams

Twinkling stars in the garden cool,
Fireflies flicker, breaking the rule.
A frog jumps high for a moonlit toast,
An airborne leap—what a merry boast!

The breeze carries whispers, oh so sly,
As rabbits plot under a pinkish sky.
With their top hats, they hop and hop,
Practicing steps on their flowered crop.

Night blooms with giggles that twirl and prance,
Every leaf knows when to dance.
A beetle winks, hurries by,
Sipping nectar, oh my oh my!

In this realm where dreams take flight,
Laughter reigns, what a lovely sight.
Amidst the fun and frolicsome gleams,
Magic lives in dappled dreams.

Beneath the Veil of Twilight

Underpurple skies, a frog recites,
His best jokes with dazzling lights.
The glowworms laugh with glee and cheer,
As crickets play their nightly gear.

Bunnies hop with a grand display,
Sporting sunglasses in the fray.
Staring down the firefly Maria,
While smooth-talking insects bring euphoria.

They twirl and tumble, beat the drum,
A concert where even the turtles strum.
With tiny crowns, they groan and roll,
"This fairy tale's lost absolute control!"

As the night rambles on, a jolly spree,
With every chuckle, the laughter's free.
In this odd dance beneath the night's face,
Every giggle leaves a soft trace.

Fragments of a Forgotten Forest

In a grove where mischief plays,
A squirrel's in a nutty craze.
Packing acorns as treasures rare,
Tripping over roots—oh, what a scare!

The trees giggle with leafy glee,
As mushrooms sway like they're free.
A wise old owl hoots, "What a sight!"
While the raccoon dances with all his might.

Echoes of laughter fill the air,
As critters plot with joyful flair.
An epic game of hidden and seek,
They tumble down, each with a squeak.

Lost in whimsy, undermoonbeams bright,
A fantastical scene in the soft twilight.
In this theater of a natural sort,
The forgotten forest holds its own court.

Rhythms of the Solitary Night

The crickets hold a concert, loud,
They've got no time for feeling proud.
The moon giggles behind a tree,
Watching squirrels dance with glee.

A raccoon wears a hat too tight,
He prances round without a fright.
The stars laugh as they wink and twirl,
While owls hoot, giving it a whirl.

The breeze sneezes, it must be cold,
A tale of mischief yet untold.
Bats play tag with a bright firefly,
The night is a stage in the sky.

So here's to nights of silly dreams,
Where laughter flows like bubbling streams.
With every chirp, snicker, and peep,
The solitary night can't help but leap.

The Heartbeat of Twilight Woods

In the woods where creatures prance,
Twilight's here to start the dance.
A chipmunk with a snazzy coat,
Tries to keep his rhythm afloat.

The trees shake leaves in cheeky glee,
As whispers pass through branches free.
Badgers join, with swagger they roam,
Together they make this place a home.

A porcupine kicks up some dust,
While squirrels giggle, that's a must.
With every rustle and silly sound,
Hilarity underfoot is found.

So let the laughter echo wide,
As creatures jive, and hearts collide.
In twilight's embrace, what a sight,
The woods come alive at night!

Longing for the Unfathomable

A starfish dreams of flying high,
While wishing on a pumpkin pie.
The sea turtles roll their eyes,
At ocean dreams beneath the skies.

A whale hums tunes of distant lands,
Meanwhile, octopuses make bands.
With ink and bubbles, they create,
A symphony that won't quite wait.

The clowns of coral dance with flair,
While seahorses twirl without care.
They long for clouds and sunny rays,
But splashy fun defines their days.

So here's to wishes that float and glide,
In realms of water, they take pride.
For what is low can aim for high,
In laughter, let their dreams comply!

The Play of Light and Shadows

The sun throws games on garden beds,
While rabbits check in from their spreads.
With floppy ears and a wink, they play,
In the dance of dusk, they sway.

A butterfly flutters in a fuss,
As shadows tease, creating a fuss.
The daisies dress in golden glow,
While night creeps in, and giggles flow.

Chasing reflections, a cat's delight,
In the tussle 'tween day and night.
With every pounce and darting glance,
The evening breezes start the dance.

So let us all join in the cheer,
For life's a jest when friends are near.
In every flicker, giggle, and fade,
Together, a merry escapade!

Where Light Falls Short

In corners where giggles like to hide,
A dance of mischief, oh, what a ride!
With secrets bolted behind dusty doors,
And laughter echoing on creaky floors.

The lamp flickers, it winks in jest,
While clumsy cats perform their best.
Each stumble a call for some wild cheer,
As shadows play games we can barely hear.

Beneath the bed, old socks take flight,
Imagination painting the night so bright.
With squeaky toys plotting a furry coup,
As night uncovers worlds we never knew.

The moon grins wide, shedding light on dirt,
While old jokes swirl like a playful flirt.
In whimsical realms where giggles abound,
We find ourselves in the joy all around.

Ephemeral Breezes in Dim Corners

In nooks and crannies, whispers take wing,
Tickling the air with each silly thing.
A breeze that knows how to tickle your nose,
As it twirls through old socks and mismatched clothes.

With dust motes dancing in lazy delight,
Forgotten toys revel in the soft light.
Each gust carries laughter wrapped in surprise,
As mysteries frolic with sparkles in eyes.

The old clock chimes, but can't keep the beat,
As nuts and bolts wiggle, oh what a feat!
In the corners where dreams dare to prance,
Even the shadows join in the dance.

Bubbles of giggles like poppies in bloom,
Sprout in the dark with a hint of perfume.
In the fading light where the silly reside,
Joy cascades down with the playful tide.

Secrets Thrumming in the Soil

Beneath our feet, a ruckus aglow,
As whispers of ants begin to bestow.
With thumpy little hearts in gardens quite grand,
Turning up mischief with each tiny hand.

A worm in a tutu twirls just for fun,
While dreams take root in the warmth of the sun.
Frogs in their chorus croak out a tune,
As giggles unfold 'neath the watchful moon.

Hidden fortunes in the dirt do lay,
Wiggly jokes waiting for the light of day.
Each pebble's a captain of adventures vast,
As laughter erupts with each bumpy blast.

The soil hums secrets, it grins with delight,
Buried treasures uncovered in playful light.
With each earthbound chuckle, the world feels whole,
As secrets spring forth, heart and soul.

Nocturnal Whispers of the Wild

In the hush of the night where giggles creep,
Creatures conspire while the world's fast asleep.
A fox in a bowtie struts through the grass,
While owls swap tales with impeccable sass.

Beneath the twinkling, a squirrel's big scheme,
Nuts are his gold in a twilight dream.
The night breeze chuckles, it sways with ease,
As shadows pirouette on moonlit leaves.

Crickets debate on a winsome note,
While raccoons giggle in a high-flying boat.
Mischief is brewing in cozy retreats,
As tales of the wild keep drumming their beats.

So hush now, dear friend, and lend a keen ear,
To the whispers of night filled with merriment dear.
In wildness, we find our chuckles and cheer,
Where laughter and mystery waltz in the clear.

The Charm of the Hidden Dell

In a glen where giggles play,
Squirrels dance and twirl away,
A frog with shades croaks out a tune,
Beneath a cheeky, purring moon.

With daisies prancing all around,
And grasshoppers in leaps abound,
A rabbit winks with mischief bright,
As butterflies take flight, just right.

A velvet breeze brings tales anew,
Of silly gnomes and fairies too,
Amidst the leaves, the jests do swell,
In this joyous hidden dell.

So let your feet skip past the thorns,
And laugh beneath the golden horns,
For in this nook, the fun won't cease,
Here's humor wrapped in nature's fleece.

Flickers of Daring Dreams

Beneath a sky of sparkling light,
A raccoon dons a helmet bright,
He dreams of ships that sail the air,
While munching snacks without a care.

The squirrels spin their daring tales,
Of pirate nuts and treasure trails,
With acorn maps and secret codes,
They dance along their leafy roads.

But when the dawn begins to break,
They nibble on their cozy cakes,
And share the dreams of night so grand,
With giggles ringing, hand in hand.

So if you see a fleet of fur,
Just know they're headed to concur,
With daring dreams that shine and gleam,
In flickers of their playful scheme.

Whims of the Whispering Woods

In the grove where secrets sigh,
An owl with glasses winks an eye,
He tells of shenanigans so sweet,
Like beetles dancing on their feet.

The trees gossip in hushed delight,
As raccoons plan their sneaky flight,
While ferns sway softly in the breeze,
Sharing quirks with the buzzing bees.

A dandy fox, with suave aplomb,
Scribbles jokes that make you calm,
He charms the critters 'neath the moon,
With whimsy scattered all in tune.

So wander deep and hear them cheer,
The playful prattle, laughter clear,
In woods where whimsy spins its lace,
Join in the fun, embrace the place.

The Covert Constellation

Up in the night where legends gleam,
A hedgehog sketches out a dream,
With starlit pools that twinkle bright,
And giggles echo in the night.

The critters gather, whispers stay,
As they paint the skies in wild array,
From tadpoles flinging twinkling light,
To fireflies buzzing with delight.

A parade of antics, oh so grand,
With laughter bouncing, hand in hand,
They play at being interstellar,
With every twirl, a cosmic jester.

So look above, make a wish or two,
For hidden laughter waits for you,
In this covert play of light and glee,
Where dreams are woven, wild and free.

The Lingering Breath of Autumn

Leaves flutter down like a clumsy ballet,
Squirrels debate if they should stay.
Sweaters emerge with a stylish flair,
Pumpkin spice lattes? Please, if you dare!

Ghosts of summer whisper with glee,
As the wind prances and teases the tree.
A dance of colors, oh what a sight,
Nature's own party, a comedic delight!

Scarecrows wobble with each playful breeze,
Wishing for crows, but just got bees.
Chilly air rolls in, a frosty prank,
Join in the laughter, let's fill up the tank!

Crisp apples chuckle, pie in their fate,
Best served warm? No need to wait!
As the days grow short, let merriment broach,
In the lingering breath, we'll never encroach!

A Serenade for the Shy

Beneath the stars, a timid tune hums,
Whispers of mischief, both gentle and glum.
Cats in the alley wear capes of pure stealth,
Plotting their antics, their nighttime wealth.

A bashful breeze nudges the leaves so light,
Like shy little dancers who hide out of sight.
Gather round, creatures of every disguise,
For even the quiet can be a surprise!

Owl's got gossip; the moon, a sly wink,
Rabbits gossip while probably think.
In night-time's arms, secrets are found,
Where laughter and shadow go round and round.

So here's to the bashful who just can't break free,
Let's croon a melody, a dazzling decree!
Though quiet may linger, don't lose the beat,
For in every giggle, shy souls are sweet!

Beneath the Veil of the Woods

In the thicket where giggles get lost,
A band of critters plans the wild cost.
With acorns as currency, they're ready to trade,
For an evening of jokes that will never fade!

A raccoon in glasses, quite wise yet bizarre,
Tells tales of adventures from here to afar.
Squirrels take notes, with comedic flair,
As the heartbeat of night fuels their wild air!

Ferns sway to laughter, the leaves join the cheer,
While crickets around them form a band sincere.
It's a raucous affair under branches so high,
As the wisdom of nature goes winging by.

So gather your courage, step into this play,
Where hilarity blossoms and shadows sway.
In halls of the woods, with each jest, we rejoice,
For laughter's the magic that gives us a voice!

The Dance of the Nocturnal Breeze

A soft chuckle drifts on the night's gentle air,
The moon's shadow dips low, with a twist of flair.
Mice in tuxedos, all ready to prance,
Hosting a soirée, an enchanting dance!

The breeze, a performer, with flair to show,
Twists and it twirls, a whimsical flow.
Beetles bring beats as they tap on their shells,
Joining the fun with soft little yells.

Whispers of crickets turn into a song,
As fireflies flicker and join in along.
A cat with a top hat arrives with a grin,
As the night bubbles over with giddy chagrin!

So sway with the laughter, let your spirits lift,
In the dance of the night, find your own special gift.
For under the stars, where silliness weaves,
The night is a canvas for all joy it leaves!

Reflections in the Half-Light

In the dimmest of glows, a dance of the bizarre,
Creatures prancing, oh, how peculiar they are!
A cat in a bow tie, sipping herbal tea,
Wearing mismatched socks, as proud as can be.

A squirrel with a top hat, plays chess with a crow,
While rabbits nearby are putting on a show.
They giggle and tumble, life's quite a feast,
In the half-light adventure, laughter won't cease.

Marshmallows are plotting a grand little heist,
As fireflies twinkle, oh, aren't they precise?
Underneath the twirls of a peculiar moon,
Expect the unexpected, it ends way too soon.

So join the odd gatherings when evening is here,
For the finest of antics, come share a good cheer!
With each quirky moment, let the giggles ignight,
In splendid reflections of whimsical night.

Whispers in the Twilight

In twilight's embrace, the world starts to sway,
Pigs in pajamas are planning to play.
Chickens with shades cluck secrets so quick,
While an owl in a tutu keeps time with a tick.

Feathers and fur, they gather around,
When the moon wears a grin, mischief abounds.
A dance-off erupts, who'll take home the crown?
As cats form a conga to boogie downtown!

The flowers are giggling, their petals all bright,
While ants in a band sing under the night.
With rhythms and rhymes, they spin tales so sly,
As whispers of whimsy are taking to fly.

So come lend an ear, to the chortles and cheer,
In the twilight's allure, there's magic so near.
Even the stars can't help but to twinkle,
In this quirky little world where dreams start to crinkle.

The Elegance of Nightfall

As nightfall arrives, with its velvet embrace,
The raccoons in tuxedos start waltzing with grace.
They twirl with the crickets, oh, what a surprise,
While the fireflies wink in their sparkly ties.

Overhead, the moon dons her lacy attire,
A ballet of clouds begins to inspire.
The frogs sing arias with only one note,
While moles in the shadows take turns on the boat.

Elegance whispers through branches so dear,
As whispers of laughter float close to your ear.
It's a swirling fiesta of chaos and class,
With every misstep, pure joy often trespass.

So when the sky darkens, don't fret or be shy,
Join the dance of the night, let your spirits fly high.
For in all its splendor, the chaos is here,
In the elegance found, joy's always sincere.

Mysteries Beneath the Canopy

Beneath the great branches, where oddities dwell,
A family of insects are casting a spell.
The ants wear top hats, and the beetles have flair,
While caterpillars conspire in whispers to share.

A hedgehog detective sorts clues with great zeal,
As toadstools in tears wish to stand with a wheel.
They concoct a potion of jelly and sass,
In hopes it will help them all dance through the grass.

The owls are amused by a circus parade,
Of squirrels on stilts who aren't simply afraid.
With a cheer and a hoot, they flip and they fly,
While laughter erupts at the slip and the sigh.

So linger awhile in this world full of glee,
Where mysteries weave through the grand canopy.
In the oddest of corners, wonders await,
For in tales of the night, there's no room for fate.

Songs of the Dusk's Embrace

In twilight's grip, a giggle stirs,
Poor crickets flee from clumsy blurs.
A dancing bat with wobbly flair,
Dresses bats in a mishap wear.

The moon chuckles, a silver orb,
At wise old owls with tales absorb.
They hoot and holler, make their stand,
While night's strange crew forms a band.

Fireflies blink like silly stars,
Playing tag with old jagged bars.
Each flicker's a jest, quite absurd,
As bugs hitch rides on a whimsical word.

With nature's quirks, a laugh we'll find,
In every step, a joke entwined.
The dusk delights in a comical chase,
And all of life wears a playful face.

The Serpent's Trail of Ambiguity

A slinky snake with a sassy grin,
Slides through tales where mischief's been.
With a wink and a nod, it curls and twirls,
Leaving giggles in the waiting world.

It whispers secrets to buzzing bees,
While frogs croak verses with clumsy ease.
Each twist and turn, a puzzle's game,
No two paths are ever the same.

The trees chuckle with rustling leaves,
As gossip blooms where no one believes.
A parade of critters joins the fun,
On this slippery road, a race begun.

In the dim light, all critters scheme,
Spinning tales that stretch and beam.
With each sly glance and playful pounce,
Who knows what trickery might announce?

A Whisper in the Foliage

Under branches, secrets breeze,
In the rustling leaves, laughter frees.
The raccoon's hat, a city's style,
Beneath the moon, it struts a while.

A fox with flair, adjusts her tail,
Crafting stories where mischief prevails.
Echoing giggles in the shady grove,
Where every nook has something to prove.

A snail debates with a racing hare,
"Who's the fastest? Fair's not fair!"
With every inch, a drawn-out jest,
This leafy lounge hosts nature's best.

And as the stars pop into view,
The night joins in with a hearty boo.
Each rustle and whisper, pure delight,
In the forest's party, all's just right.

Uncharted Realms of the Night

In night's embrace, strange things unfurl,
While giggles twine like a glittering pearl.
Invisible capers on frosty air,
As silly sprites test their cheeky flair.

With every step, the world may quake,
'Did you hear that?' echoes, a sneak peek break.
Underneath stars, a game's in play,
As laughter drips like dew at bay.

Wandering shadows, they bump and shake,
Chasing their tails for fun's sweet sake.
Twinkling eyes in the pitch-dark spin,
Hide and seek, where giggles begin.

In uncharted lands, it's all a jest,
With whimsy blooming, never a rest.
So follow the mirth, let laughter take flight,
In the mystic dance of an enchanted night.

The Lure of Lingering Haze

In the fog, the cats look sly,
Pouncing whispers as they try.
Laughter twirls in smoky air,
As secrets dance without a care.

Jokes float like bubbles in the night,
Chasing dreams just out of sight.
Wit wraps around like a warm embrace,
Tickling fancies in a silly race.

What hides behind the puffs and curls?
A world of giggles, twirls, and swirls.
With each step, a jest is made,
As lightness wins in this charade.

The haze may play a sneaky game,
But all that glitters is not the same.
In the mist, find joy and sass,
For life is fun when you let it pass.

Silhouettes in the Moonlight

Under the glow, the figures prance,
Swaying gently, lost in chance.
Ghostly giggles fill the air,
As mischief brews with playful flair.

A shadow dips, a shadow leaps,
While laughter echoes, softly creeps.
In the moon's glow, secrets unfold,
With jokes spun bright and stories told.

Eerie shapes in silly poses,
Chasing laughs like blooming roses.
Each twist and turn, a dance of glee,
In the night, we're wild and free.

Let the dark play tricks and tease,
For in this night, we do as we please.
Wit sparkles bright, like stars above,
In humor's arms, we'll always love.

The Essence of Flickering Ember

Little sparks glow in the dark,
Crackling laughter, a cheerful lark.
They snap and pop like a song in flight,
As friends gather 'round, hearts feeling light.

Crimson hues dance in the night,
Chasing away all hints of fright.
Jokes take flight with a whoosh and a boom,
Creating warmth in the gathering gloom.

With each flicker of flame's debate,
A punchline waits with mischievous fate.
Stories whirl like firefly spins,
Lighting up faces with chortles and grins.

So pass the marshmallows, let's toast and cheer,
This cozy gathering brings joy near.
In the heat, we find unexpected bliss,
With every wink, we seal a kiss.

A Tangle of Unseen Roots

Beneath the soil, pockets of glee,
Tickling laughter, no one can see.
Buried deep where the laughter lies,
Roots entwined with clever replies.

Sneaky whispers from below,
Crafting fun in a rootsy show.
With every twist and every turn,
Secrets sprout as we brightly yearn.

Mischief blooms with every dig,
In this garden, nothing's too big.
Jokes take root, then grow so wide,
Underneath, where good times abide.

So let's explore this playful space,
Where humor finds its own embrace.
In tangled dreams where smiles sprout,
Life's quirks are what it's all about.

The Playful Gaze of the Evening Star

Up above, a wink and a smile,
The day's gone, but not for a while.
Planets giggle, start to play,
Nighttime shenanigans on display.

Comets tease with a flash of light,
"Catch us if you can!" they take flight.
Constellations dance in a swirl,
A cosmic party, let's give it a twirl.

Laughter echoing from afar,
A mischievous wink from the evening star.
While crickets chirp their nightly song,
With every note, the fun grows long.

"Who can leap higher?" the moonlight dares,
While fireflies twinkle without cares.
The world below, a quiet chuckle,
As zany dreams take shape and buckle.

In the Realm of Hidden Whispers

In a glen where secrets play,
The trees gossip, come what may.
Ferns unfold their leafy ears,
Catching tales through subtle sneers.

A breeze giggles, stirring the air,
Rustling leaves with style and flair.
The ground-hugging moss joins in the fun,
As mushrooms chuckle beneath the sun.

Privacy's a game to these clever sprites,
Playing hide and seek among the nights.
With every rustle, they stifle a snort,
Nature's comedy, a timeless sport.

"Did you hear that?" a whisper suggests,
As the world around plays dress-up quests.
In this enchanted, giggling space,
Every shadow hides a laugh's embrace.

The Allure of Timid Trysts

Underneath a rosy sky,
Two kindred spirits pass on by.
With shy glances and suppressed grins,
They circle 'round, where laughter begins.

In a garden where blushing blooms rise,
A bashful plot weaves crafty ties.
Petals flutter, caught in the fray,
As whispers linger and dance and sway.

"Shall we hold hands?" the bravest might joke,
As leaves flutter and softly invoke.
Tickled by breezes, they take to the lane,
With every step, their giggles remain.

A stolen glance, a shy retreat,
With every heartbeat, they skip a beat.
In the twilight glow, romance unfolds.
Timid tales of laughter, lightly told.

Enigmatic Echoes of the Wild

In the depth of the woods, where laughter swells,
Creatures chatter and weave their spells.
Whiskers twitch with gleeful thrill,
As critters plot with comedic skill.

The owls wink from their lofty throne,
Sharing secrets in a hushed tone.
While squirrels conspire in playful glee,
My, what a humorous cacophony!

"Shhh, here comes the curious hare!"
Psst! What's that? Is it aware?
Feathers ruffle, and shadows caper,
In this wild stage, laughter's the paper.

With every rustle, a punchline grows,
The trees sway gently, as wisdom flows.
The enchantment of mischief unfolds the night,
In this world of giggles, all feels just right.

The Art of Whispered Narratives

In corners where secrets dare to play,
The banter of leaves in a giddy ballet.
With every rustle, a chuckle adds flair,
The stories unfold in the breeze with a stare.

A squirrel's grand tale of a nut on the run,
Told by a toad who basked in the sun.
Oh, listen closely to their merry spree,
Each whisper a giggle, wild and free!

The moon winks slyly, gains glimmers of fun,
As fireflies twinkle, the night has begun.
Chasing each shadow, they dance with delight,
A carnival of chatter under starlit night.

So come take a seat 'neath the gossiping trees,
Where gales get all giddy and tumble with ease!
Each creature is keen with a laugh-up-the-sleeve,
In the art of whispers, we dance and believe.

Enchantment Entwined in Nature

When blossoms giggle beneath the warm sun,
And branches gossip, oh what fun!
The breeze carries jokes, both silly and bright,
Caressing the flowers in soft, pure delight.

A rabbit hops in, with mischief in mind,
Stealing a carrot, oh how unrefined!
With wise old owls pondering at night,
The woodland joins in, sharing laughter and light.

Mushrooms wear hats, all floppy and wide,
Their caps droop down like a friendly guide.
While crickets compose their symphony loud,
The dance of the forest draws in quite a crowd.

So take a deep breath in this whimsical space,
Where every leaf shimmers with giggles and grace.
Nature's a jester, so don't be a bore,
Step softly, dear friend; there's laughter in store.

The Last Breath of Daylight

As evening tiptoes, the world starts to blend,
With chuckles of critters, they'll never pretend.
Stars giggle softly, their twinkle a jest,
While day's tired sighs are met with a jest.

The sun throws a wink, bidding goodnight,
While shadows frolic; oh what a sight!
The rabbit moon beams from high in the sky,
Whispering tales as the fireflies fly.

The grass waves hello with a playful swoosh,
As night breaks the dance in a giggly push.
Cicadas hum songs to carry the tune,
A serenade sweet from dusk 'til the moon.

So gather your dreams ere the light takes a bow,
In the laughter of dusk, don't forget how!
For every last shadow brings joy to the night,
A tapestry woven with giggles and light.

A Journey into the Twilight's Heart

Strolling 'neath the twilight, where the sky meets the ground,
The air fills with chuckles, a whimsical sound.
With each step we take, the world starts to spin,
As the day's great adventures are wearing thin.

A cat on the fence gives a stretch and a yawn,
With tales of his romps, from dusk until dawn.
His whiskers dance lightly, like notes in a song,
Every flick of his tail says, 'Come along!'

The coyotes croon softly, a chorus of cheer,
Their voices like velvet, enchanting the ear.
The sky dons a blush as the stars start to peek,
Inviting you closer, to giggle and sneak.

So join this adventure where whimsy takes flight,
In the heart of the dusk, all aglow with delight!
Where every sweet moment is playful, yet wise,
A journey of fun beneath twinkling skies.

Secrets Woven in Twilight

In the dusk where the giggles dwell,
Squirrels plot with a secret shell.
Whispers bounce on the twilight breeze,
Dancing giggling through the trees.

Bats wear tiny capes to fly,
While owls wear glasses, oh so sly.
The moon winks, a comical sight,
As fireflies join the silly plight.

Rabbits on pogo sticks jump high,
While frogs croak jokes that make you cry.
The stars above twinkle in cheer,
As the night hums in giggles near.

But when the dawn begins to glow,
All the silly secrets go.
Yet in dreams, we'll surely find,
Those cheeky whispers left behind.

The Spirit of the Unseen Forest

In the woods where the laughter thrives,
Critters don capes, living their lives.
Wily foxes play pranks so dear,
While raccoons steal chips without fear.

Mushrooms throw a fancy ball,
Blooms in hats try not to fall.
Sassy squirrels steal the show,
With tiny boots and a little bow.

The breeze giggles with every rustle,
Trees wear whispers, full of bustle.
A spirit flits, a charming guide,
Through the fun that nature provides.

As twilight fades, they bid adieu,
With a wink and a chuckle, it's true.
Though the night falls with seems so stark,
The forest knows it's just a lark.

The Cryptic Dance of Night

When the moon grins wide and bright,
Creatures gather for a silly plight.
Ghosts with jigs and a twisty spin,
Invite the stars to join in.

Witches brew a bubbling stew,
While owls hoot a cheerful tune.
With broomsticks adorned with candy canes,
They laugh away their worries and pains.

A shadow slips, a playful tease,
As raccoons throw their hands and freeze.
The night takes on a comical flair,
With echoes of giggles filling the air.

As dawn approaches, they take a bow,
Saying "Until next time, here and now!"
Leaving the night with stories grand,
Of their dance, across the land.

Unveiling the Hidden Narrative

In the murky twilight out they creep,
With tales to share that make you leap.
Unfurling secrets with every glance,
Little creatures join the dance.

The wise old tree, a storyteller,
Whispers jokes, a wordy feller.
While hedgehogs in tutus twirl about,
With so much laughter, there's no doubt.

The grass tickles toes as fairies blink,
They brew up joy in a fun, warm drink.
Each tale brings smiles, each giggle a cheer,
As laughter ricochets, near and dear.

So gather 'round as night unfolds,
And listen close to what the forest holds.
For in the murmur of joyous lore,
Lives a mirth, forevermore.

A Serenade to the Unseen

In corners where the giggles hide,
They tickle leaves, on mischief ride.
A rustle here, a whisper there,
As if the night holds secrets rare.

With giggles soft, and sways so slight,
They dance in pairs, such a delight.
An owl looks on, a wink he gives,
While all around, the mischief lives.

The fireflies join in with a twinkle,
As laughter blends with a little sprinkle.
The unseen guests play tricks with glee,
Inviting all to join their spree.

The Brush of Gentle Nightfall

When day departs and quirks arise,
The world becomes a canvas wide.
Pencil lines of antics drawn,
Fill every nook at the break of dawn.

A cheeky breeze, a wink of fate,
Makes critters dance, oh what a state!
They twirl like tops, they spin and skip,
Around the roots, a playful trip.

As stars do glimmer with goofy flair,
Creatures frolic without a care.
In rhythmic beats, they leap and prance,
Night falls gently, a reveling dance.

The Mystery of the Woodland Veil

Beneath the leaves of shifting hues,
Are giggling whispers, tangled cues.
A riddle sprawls with every twirl,
As sneaky elves in shadows whirl.

A toadstool throne holds a tiny king,
Who dodges raindrops like it's a fling.
The ferns wave hands in a sneaky jest,
As creatures of the night feel blessed.

With each rustle hides a prank,
A leafy joke in a cozy bank.
In this strange woods, tales intertwine,
As chuckling laughter breezes divine.

Glimmers of Light in the Thicket

In tangled brambles, a light does flick,
A trail of giggles, quick and slick.
Under the moon, they weave and bound,
As playmates frolic on the ground.

Like mischief makers, bold and bright,
They plot their schemes with sheer delight.
A squirrel peeks with a knowing grin,
As friends unite in a dance to begin.

With winks and nods, the night unfolds,
Whispers exchanged that never grow old.
In every glimmer, joy does find,
A sprinkle of laughter, sweet and kind.

A Chronicle of Lost Hours

In the garden where time slips through,
Gnomes gossip 'bout the things they knew,
A squirrel scurries, steals a shoe,
While daisies giggle in morning dew.

Lily pads dress in their finest green,
A frog declares he reigns as king,
With a crown made of twigs, who'd ever glean?
The dance of the bees is a hilarious thing.

Butterflies wield their vibrant wit,
Chasing dreams until they flit,
A ladybug claims she must admit,
Her new polka dots are a pure hit!

The clock strikes noon, the party's begun,
Where grasshoppers play jokes and run,
But as the day fades, oh what a pun,
Lost hours vanish, the laughter's done!

An Intrigue Wrapped in Green

In the thicket where secrets lie tight,
A raccoon digs for a snack at night,
With a blueberry hat, what a comical sight,
He's plotting mischief with all his might.

The ivy whispers to the old oak tree,
'Tell me a tale of your great jubilee!'
The tree chuckles softly, 'Just wait and see,
For birds steal my wisdom, how rude can they be?'

A caterpillar bursts into song,
Lamenting how the world feels wrong,
He sways with style, oh so strong,
Yet still munches leaves—what a throng!

Just when you think the plot's at rest,
A zebra-striped lizard shows up, quite dressed,
He claims he's a spy on an urgent quest,
But really just wants to join the jest!

Secrets of the Quiet Glade

In a hush where the creatures conspire,
An owl hoots, 'Oh, retire!'
While rabbits squeak of an ancient flyer,
That promises gags to lift you higher.

The mushrooms roll their eyes in jest,
As crickets insist they're the best guest,
With karaoke nights, no need for rest,
While fireflies twinkle in matching vests.

A chipmunk balances nuts with flair,
Proclaiming he's the acorn heir,
Yet stumbles on roots—oh, what a scare!
His friends all giggle, so light and rare.

As the stars twinkle, the stories unwind,
With each chuckle, a new twist is designed,
Nature's humor, perfectly aligned,
In the glade where silliness is kind.

Hidden Melodies of the Forest

What tunes are played by the pipes of dew?
The wind carries notes, both fresh and new,
As hedgehogs twirl in a merry queue,
While frogs croak verses, a catchy crew.

The branches sway with a playful song,
Tales of travelers who wandered along,
A raccoon strums a stringed tale so strong,
You'll laugh 'til morning, where you belong.

Through dappled light, mischief may bloom,
As owls sing bits of ancient cartoon,
With beetles tap-dancing to banish the gloom,
They know how fun can dispel any doom.

When night falls, the fireflies will wink,
Inviting all critters to share a drink,
Their lanterns aglow, a collective blink,
Those melodies hidden will make you think!

The Lure of Twilight's Glade

In the glade where whispers play,
Trees wear costumes by the Bay.
A squirrel dons a tiny hat,
As crickets chirp, "Well, how about that?"

Beneath the bushes, giggles swell,
A raccoon trip, oh what a spell!
With mischief wrapped in leafy green,
It's a costume party, sight unseen.

Frogs croak tunes that make us laugh,
As owls critique the silly staff.
Each leaf a dancer, bold and spry,
While moonlight twirls, oh my, oh my!

So join the feast of nature's jest,
In twilight's glade, we find our best.
Where laughter blooms and joy ascends,
In this enchanted place, dear friends.

Lament of the Moonlit Foliage

Oh, the trees lament tonight,
For bugs who think they're quite the sight.
A firefly showed off its glow,
Then tripped on roots, what a show!

The bushes giggle with a rustle,
While hedgehogs engage in a tussle.
"Did you see that owl?" they pry,
"Who hoots like it's a lullaby!"

Each petal caught a little joke,
Whispers played beneath the oak.
The moonlight nods, "I see what's here,"
As laughter fills the nighttime clear.

So we'll dance with leaves that twine,
And make a racket, oh so fine!
In foliage where spirits tease,
Our jovial hearts will find their ease.

Beneath the Boughs of Dread

What's lurking under leafy dread?
A rabbit in a hat, so misled!
With carrot jokes that make us cringe,
He hops and tumbles near the fringe.

Beneath the boughs, a shadow stirs,
"Is it a ghost?" someone concurs.
But then a raccoon with a snack,
Swaps gaze with friends, it's time to quack!

The branches creak in giggling glee,
They gossip 'bout the old pine tree.
"Did you hear what the crow just said?
He's always wrong, this talk's widespread!"

So join the fun beneath the gloom,
Where quirks and quirks, like flowers bloom.
In this realm where weird embraces,
We find our joy in funny faces.

Serendipity Among the Thickets

Among the thickets, treasures hide,
A chubby chipmunk takes a glide.
With munchies clutched like hidden gold,
He struts along, so brave, so bold!

A wild hedgehog sings a tune,
Under the bright, bemused stars' moon.
While with a wink, a laughing hare,
Plays hide and seek, without a care.

Each pebble tells a funny tale,
Of encounters that never fail.
As we discover, step by step,
The wonders in the wild's inept.

So climb the hill and join the game,
Where serendipity's never lame.
In thickets lush, let antics reign,
And joyous hearts break every chain.

www.ingramcontent.com/pod-product-compliance
Lightning Source LLC
Chambersburg PA
CBHW072141200426
43209CB00051B/254